SUPER CUTE!

Baby
Turtles

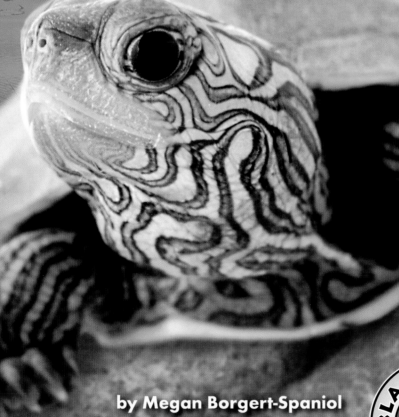

by Megan Borgert-Spaniol

BLASTOFF! READERS

BELLWETHER MEDIA • MINNEAPOLIS, MN

Note to Librarians, Teachers, and Parents:

Blastoff! Readers are carefully developed by literacy experts and combine standards-based content with developmentally appropriate text.

Level 1 provides the most support through repetition of high-frequency words, light text, predictable sentence patterns, and strong visual support.

Level 2 offers early readers a bit more challenge through varied simple sentences, increased text load, and less repetition of high-frequency words.

Level 3 advances early-fluent readers toward fluency through increased text and concept load, less reliance on visuals, longer sentences, and more literary language.

Level 4 builds reading stamina by providing more text per page, increased use of punctuation, greater variation in sentence patterns, and increasingly challenging vocabulary.

Level 5 encourages children to move from "learning to read" to "reading to learn" by providing even more text, varied writing styles, and less familiar topics.

Whichever book is right for your reader, Blastoff! Readers are the perfect books to build confidence and encourage a love of reading that will last a lifetime!

This edition first published in 2017 by Bellwether Media, Inc.

No part of this publication may be reproduced in whole or in part without written permission of the publisher. For information regarding permission, write to Bellwether Media, Inc., Attention: Permissions Department, 5357 Penn Avenue South, Minneapolis, MN 55419.

Library of Congress Cataloging-in-Publication Data

Names: Borgert-Spaniol, Megan, 1989- author.
Title: Baby Turtles / by Megan Borgert-Spaniol.
Other titles: Blastoff! Readers. 1, Super Cute!
Description: Minneapolis, MN : Bellwether Media, Inc., [2017] | Series:
    Blastoff! Readers. Super Cute! | Audience: Ages 5-8. | Audience: K to
    grade 3. | Includes bibliographical references and index.
Identifiers: LCCN 2015043282 | ISBN 9781626173903 (hardcover : alk. paper)
Subjects: LCSH: Turtles–Infancy–Juvenile literature.
Classification: LCC QL666.C5 B584 2017 | DDC 597.92/139–dc23
LC record available at http://lccn.loc.gov/2015043282

Printed in the United States of America, North Mankato, MN.

Table of Contents

Turtle Hatchling!

A baby turtle is called a hatchling. It **hatches** from an egg.

The egg is part of a **clutch**. There can be more than 100 eggs in a clutch!

Some hatchlings
live with their mom.
She lets them ride
on her back.

Many hatchlings live on their own. They watch out for hungry birds or crabs.

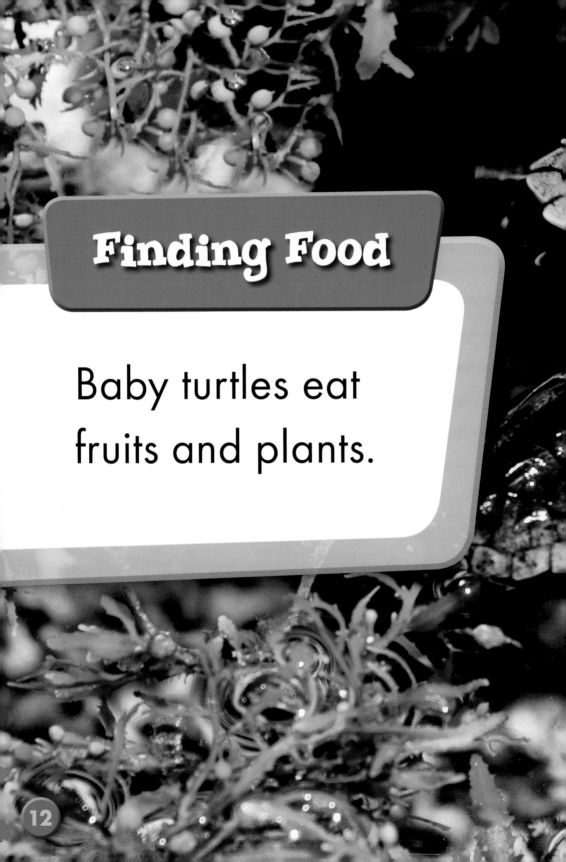

Finding Food

Baby turtles eat fruits and plants.

Some also eat **insects**, worms, and other animals.

Swimming

Most baby turtles are good swimmers. **Webbed feet** help many move through water.

webbed foot

Some turtles have **flippers**. They spend most of their lives in water.

flipper

Baby turtles **bask** on logs and rocks to stay warm. The sun feels good!

Glossary

bask—to warm the body in the sun

clutch—a group of eggs that are laid at the same time

flippers—wide, flat legs and arms that help turtles move through water

hatches—breaks out of an egg

insects—small animals with six legs and hard outer bodies; insect bodies are divided into three parts.

webbed feet—feet with thin skin that connects the toes

To Learn More

AT THE LIBRARY

Green, Emily. *Turtles*. Minneapolis, Minn.:
Bellwether Media, 2011.

Marsh, Laura F. *Sea Turtles*. Washington, D.C.:
National Geographic, 2011.

Sayre, April Pulley. *Turtle, Turtle, Watch Out!*
Watertown, Mass.: Charlesbridge, 2010.

ON THE WEB

Learning more about
turtles is as easy as 1, 2, 3.

1. Go to www.factsurfer.com.

2. Enter "turtles" into the search box.

3. Click the "Surf" button and you will see a
   list of related web sites.

With factsurfer.com, finding more information
is just a click away.

Index